These Ideas Belong to:

____

www.ingramcontent.com/pod-product-compliance
Lightning Source LLC
Chambersburg PA
CBHW081437250726
48662CB00009B/2839